J   5594940
746.9   16.95
Bak
Baker
Fashion

DATE DUE			

HANDS-ON
fashion

Wendy Baker

Author: Diane James

A **TWO-CAN** BOOK
published by
THOMSON LEARNING
New York

5594940

Contents

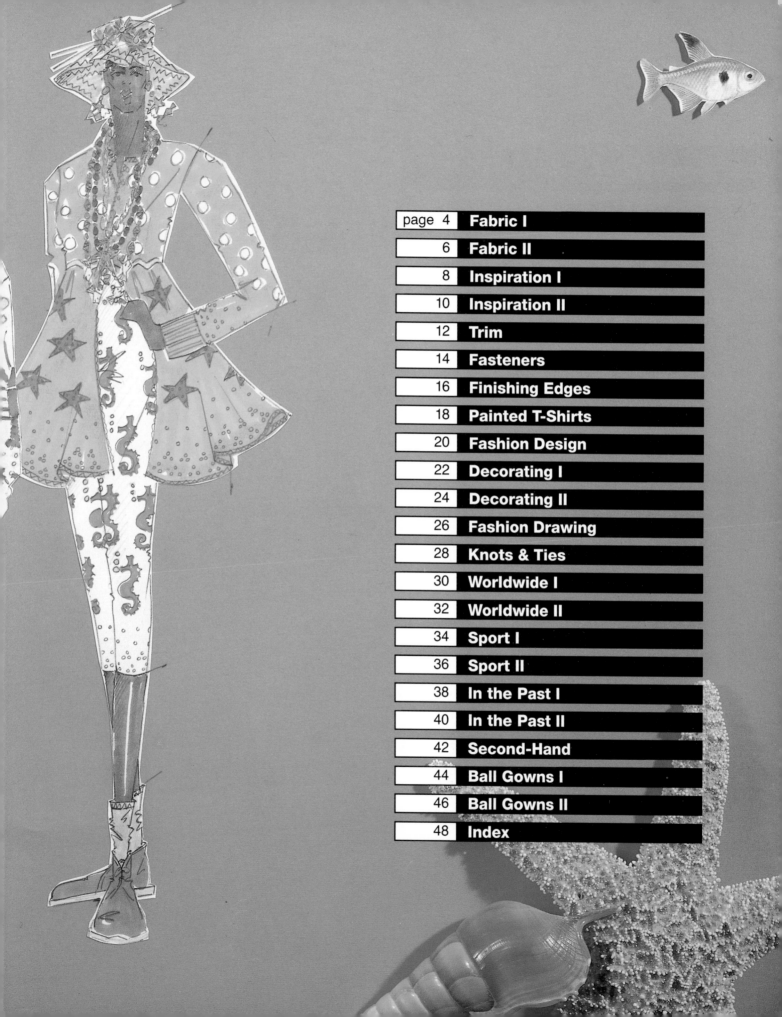

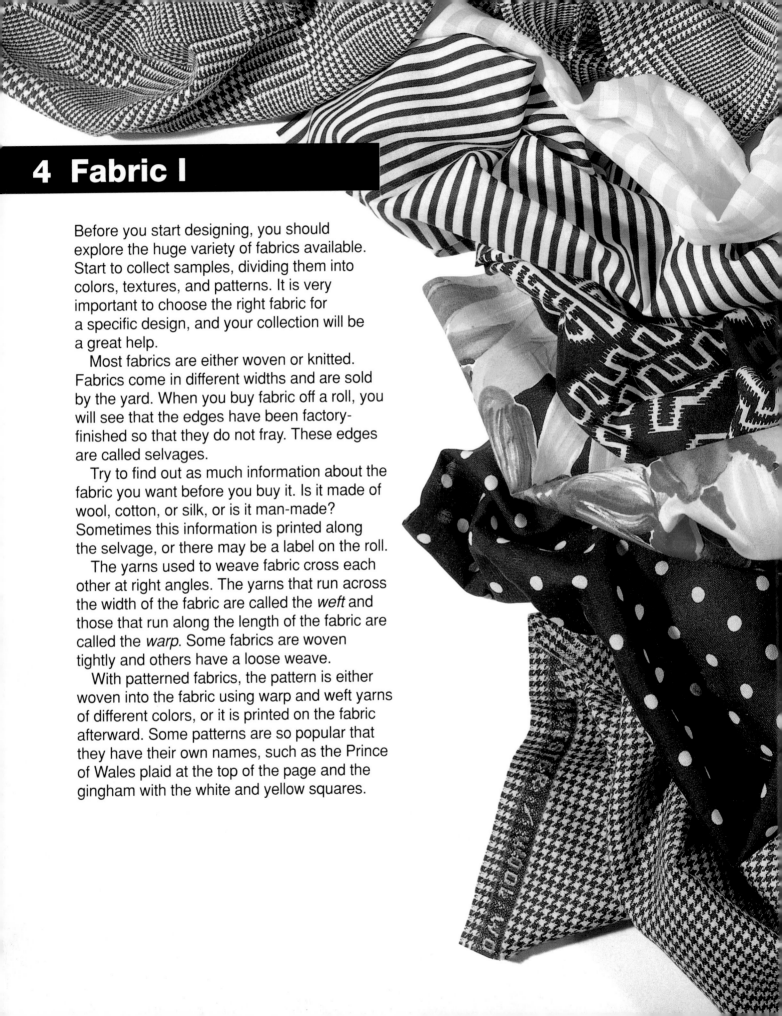

4 Fabric I

Before you start designing, you should explore the huge variety of fabrics available. Start to collect samples, dividing them into colors, textures, and patterns. It is very important to choose the right fabric for a specific design, and your collection will be a great help.

Most fabrics are either woven or knitted. Fabrics come in different widths and are sold by the yard. When you buy fabric off a roll, you will see that the edges have been factory-finished so that they do not fray. These edges are called selvages.

Try to find out as much information about the fabric you want before you buy it. Is it made of wool, cotton, or silk, or is it man-made? Sometimes this information is printed along the selvage, or there may be a label on the roll.

The yarns used to weave fabric cross each other at right angles. The yarns that run across the width of the fabric are called the *weft* and those that run along the length of the fabric are called the *warp*. Some fabrics are woven tightly and others have a loose weave.

With patterned fabrics, the pattern is either woven into the fabric using warp and weft yarns of different colors, or it is printed on the fabric afterward. Some patterns are so popular that they have their own names, such as the Prince of Wales plaid at the top of the page and the gingham with the white and yellow squares.

6 Fabric II

The fabrics here show just how much variety there is to choose from – even within a single color!

The texture of a fabric depends on the yarns used to weave it. Wool is usually soft and slightly hairy, while cotton is generally crisp and smooth. Some fabrics are woven with a mixture of different yarns, such as wool and cotton. Sometimes a special finish is added to the fabric after weaving – velvet is an example of this.

Man-made fabrics, such as polyester and acrylic, are easy to wash and do not crease as much as wool and cotton.

When you are designing, it is important to choose the most suitable fabric for your design. For example, a tough cotton fabric, such as denim, will not fall into soft folds, and a fabric that needs dry cleaning would not be the best choice for clothes designed to be worn every day.

8 Inspiration I

If you are constantly on the lookout for ideas and inspiration you will sometimes find them in the strangest places. One way to start the creative process is to pick a theme that interests you. Collect as much visual material as you can – photographs, newspaper and magazine clippings, postcards, and any other interesting odds and ends. Make a display of your findings and start thinking about the objects in relation to clothes, concentrating on shapes, texture, and color. Look at page 20 to see how this display of kitchen utensils inspired a designer.

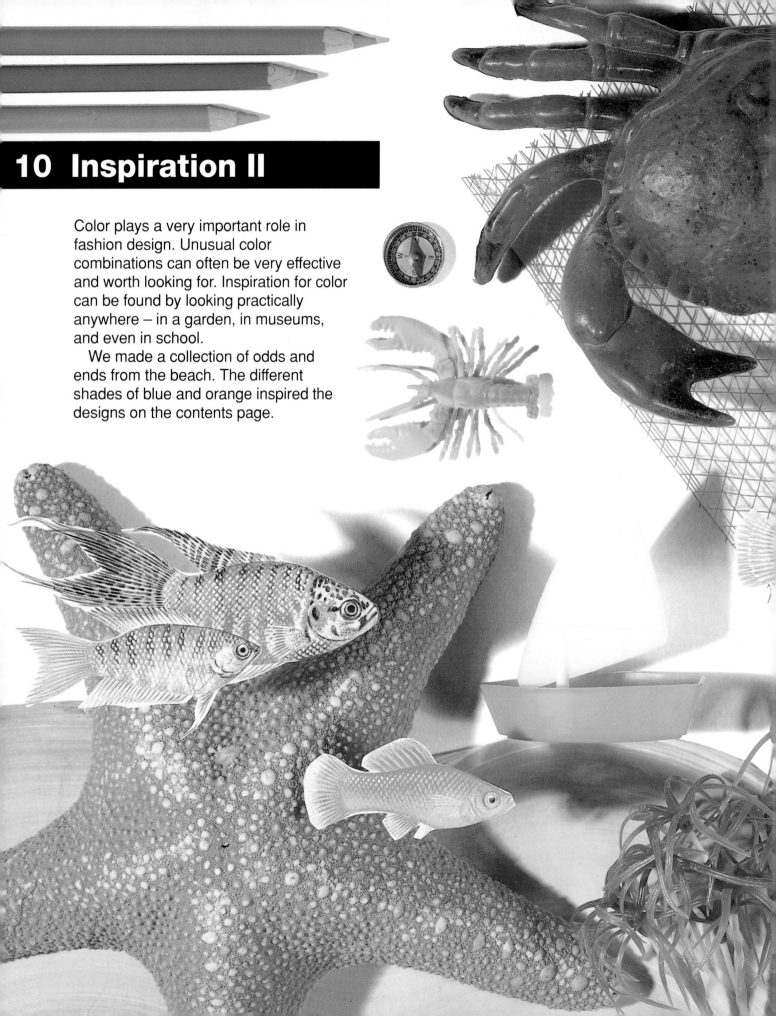

10 Inspiration II

Color plays a very important role in fashion design. Unusual color combinations can often be very effective and worth looking for. Inspiration for color can be found by looking practically anywhere – in a garden, in museums, and even in school.

We made a collection of odds and ends from the beach. The different shades of blue and orange inspired the designs on the contents page.

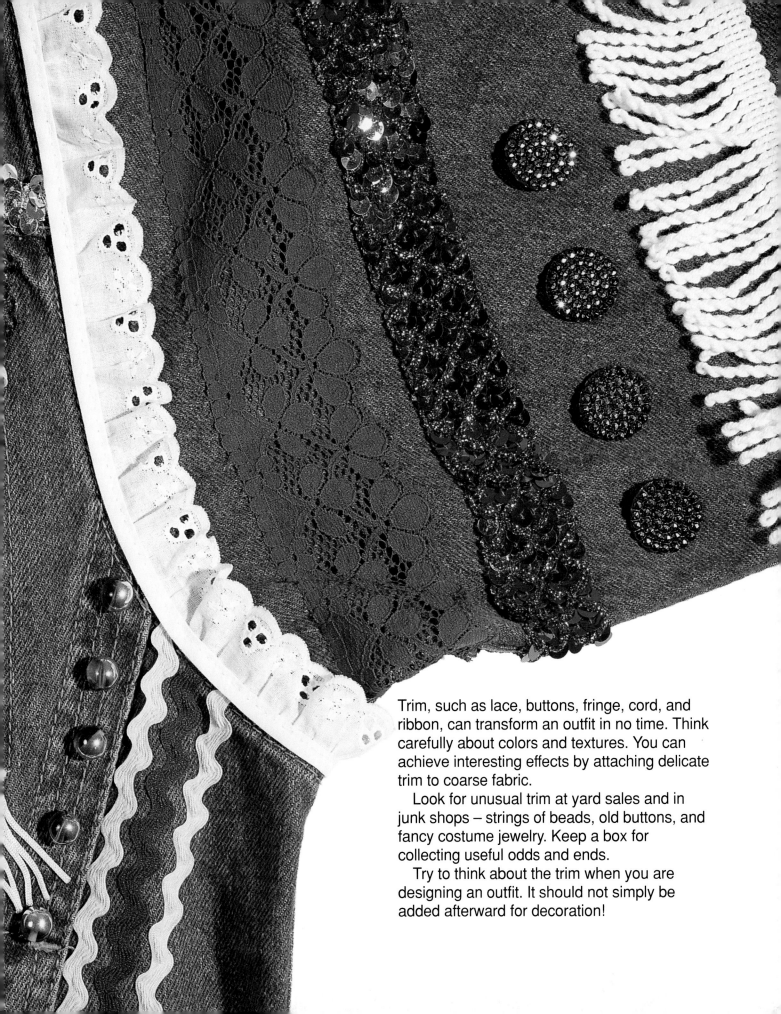

Trim, such as lace, buttons, fringe, cord, and ribbon, can transform an outfit in no time. Think carefully about colors and textures. You can achieve interesting effects by attaching delicate trim to coarse fabric.

Look for unusual trim at yard sales and in junk shops – strings of beads, old buttons, and fancy costume jewelry. Keep a box for collecting useful odds and ends.

Try to think about the trim when you are designing an outfit. It should not simply be added afterward for decoration!

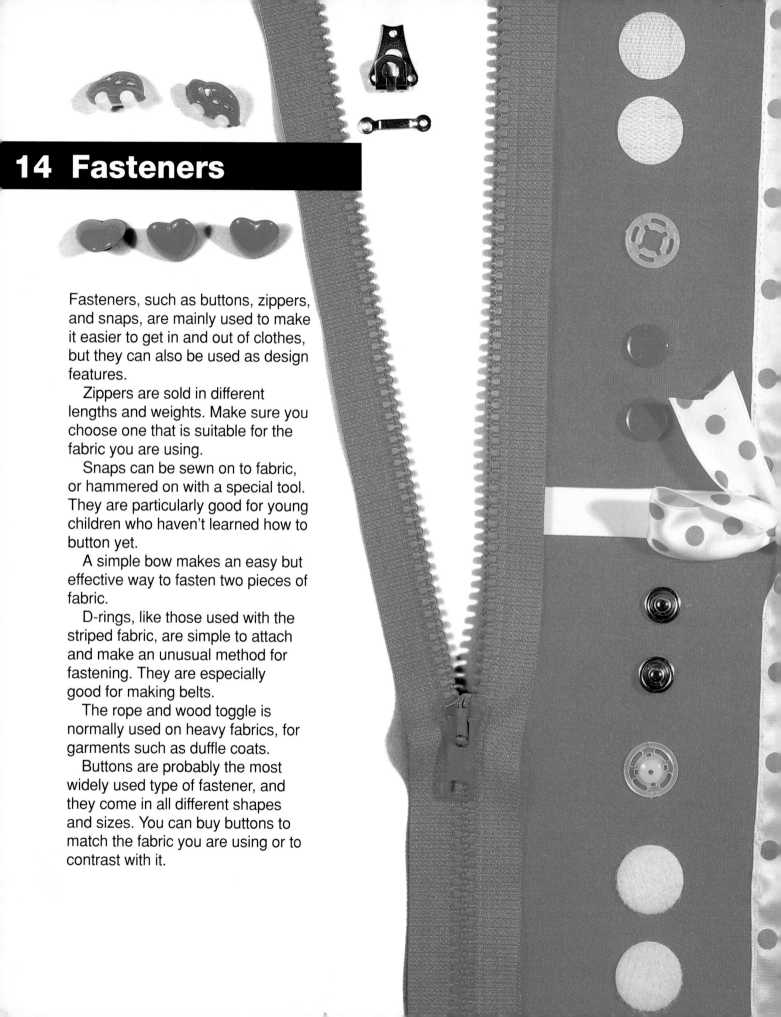

14 Fasteners

Fasteners, such as buttons, zippers, and snaps, are mainly used to make it easier to get in and out of clothes, but they can also be used as design features.

Zippers are sold in different lengths and weights. Make sure you choose one that is suitable for the fabric you are using.

Snaps can be sewn on to fabric, or hammered on with a special tool. They are particularly good for young children who haven't learned how to button yet.

A simple bow makes an easy but effective way to fasten two pieces of fabric.

D-rings, like those used with the striped fabric, are simple to attach and make an unusual method for fastening. They are especially good for making belts.

The rope and wood toggle is normally used on heavy fabrics, for garments such as duffle coats.

Buttons are probably the most widely used type of fastener, and they come in all different shapes and sizes. You can buy buttons to match the fabric you are using or to contrast with it.

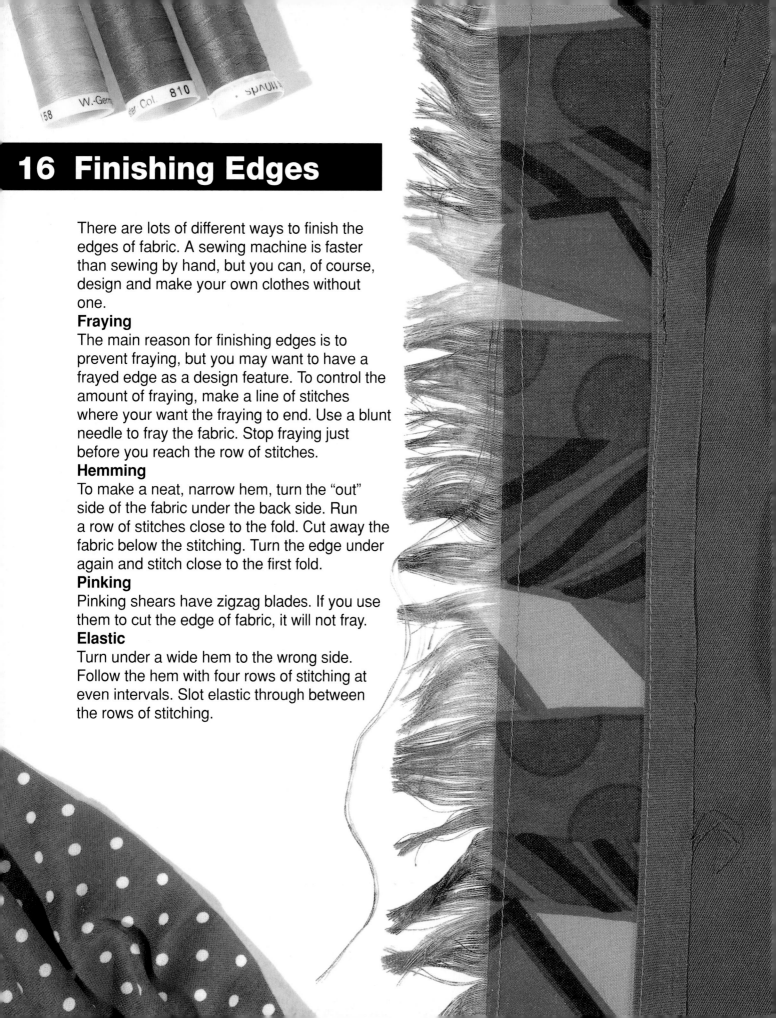

16 Finishing Edges

There are lots of different ways to finish the edges of fabric. A sewing machine is faster than sewing by hand, but you can, of course, design and make your own clothes without one.

Fraying

The main reason for finishing edges is to prevent fraying, but you may want to have a frayed edge as a design feature. To control the amount of fraying, make a line of stitches where your want the fraying to end. Use a blunt needle to fray the fabric. Stop fraying just before you reach the row of stitches.

Hemming

To make a neat, narrow hem, turn the "out" side of the fabric under the back side. Run a row of stitches close to the fold. Cut away the fabric below the stitching. Turn the edge under again and stitch close to the first fold.

Pinking

Pinking shears have zigzag blades. If you use them to cut the edge of fabric, it will not fray.

Elastic

Turn under a wide hem to the wrong side. Follow the hem with four rows of stitching at even intervals. Slot elastic through between the rows of stitching.

18 Painted T-Shirts

T-shirts in some shape or size are always in style. Printed T-shirts are usually more expensive than plain ones and it may be difficult to find the colors or design you want. The answer is to design and print your own. Use fabric paints so the design will be permanent, and read the instructions before you start.

Sketch your design first and decide what colors you want to use. Cut stencils for each color and use a stencil brush to apply the paint. Try using elements from your T-shirt design to make matching socks, scarves, hats, or even canvas shoes.

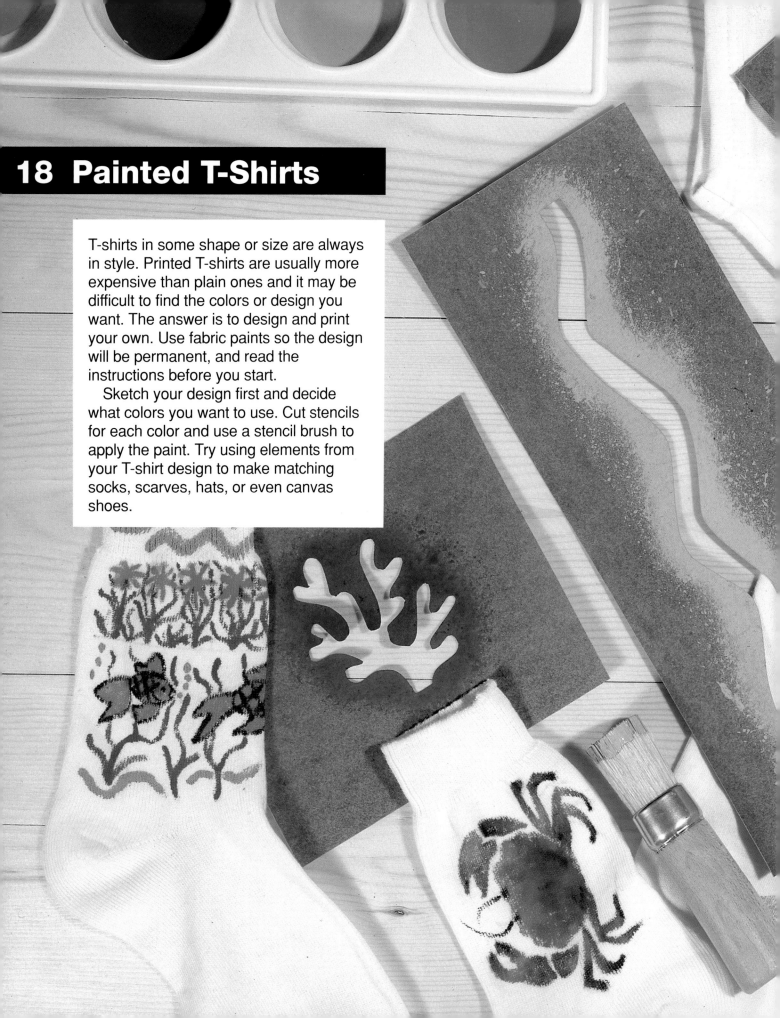

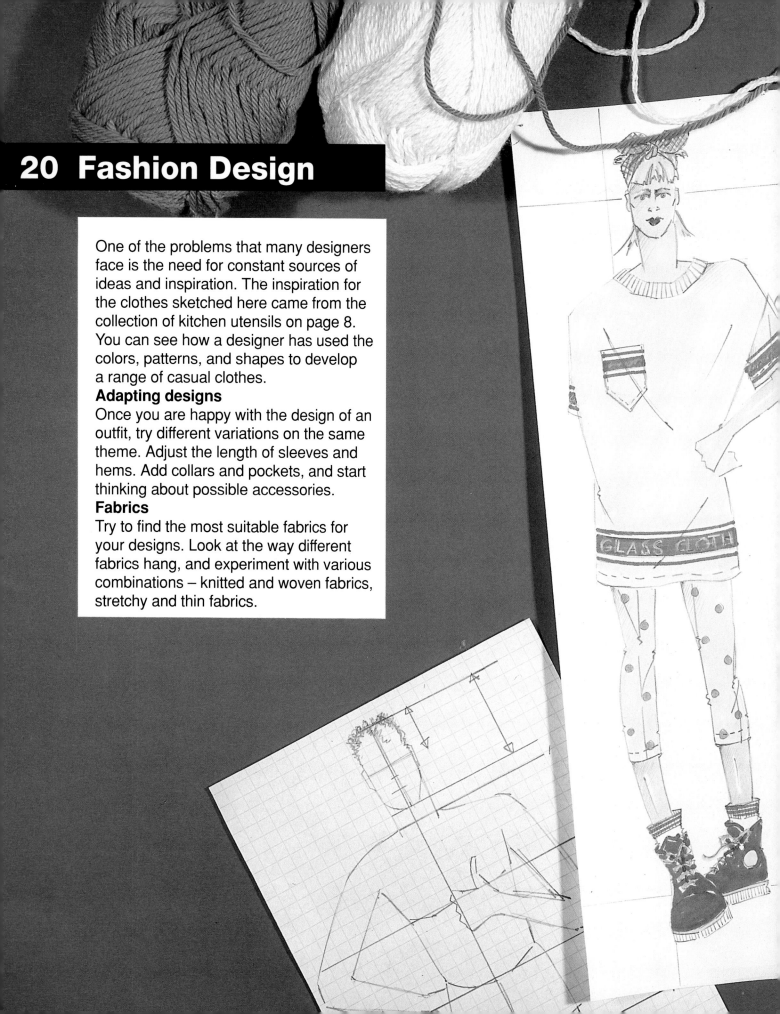

20 Fashion Design

One of the problems that many designers face is the need for constant sources of ideas and inspiration. The inspiration for the clothes sketched here came from the collection of kitchen utensils on page 8. You can see how a designer has used the colors, patterns, and shapes to develop a range of casual clothes.

Adapting designs

Once you are happy with the design of an outfit, try different variations on the same theme. Adjust the length of sleeves and hems. Add collars and pockets, and start thinking about possible accessories.

Fabrics

Try to find the most suitable fabrics for your designs. Look at the way different fabrics hang, and experiment with various combinations – knitted and woven fabrics, stretchy and thin fabrics.

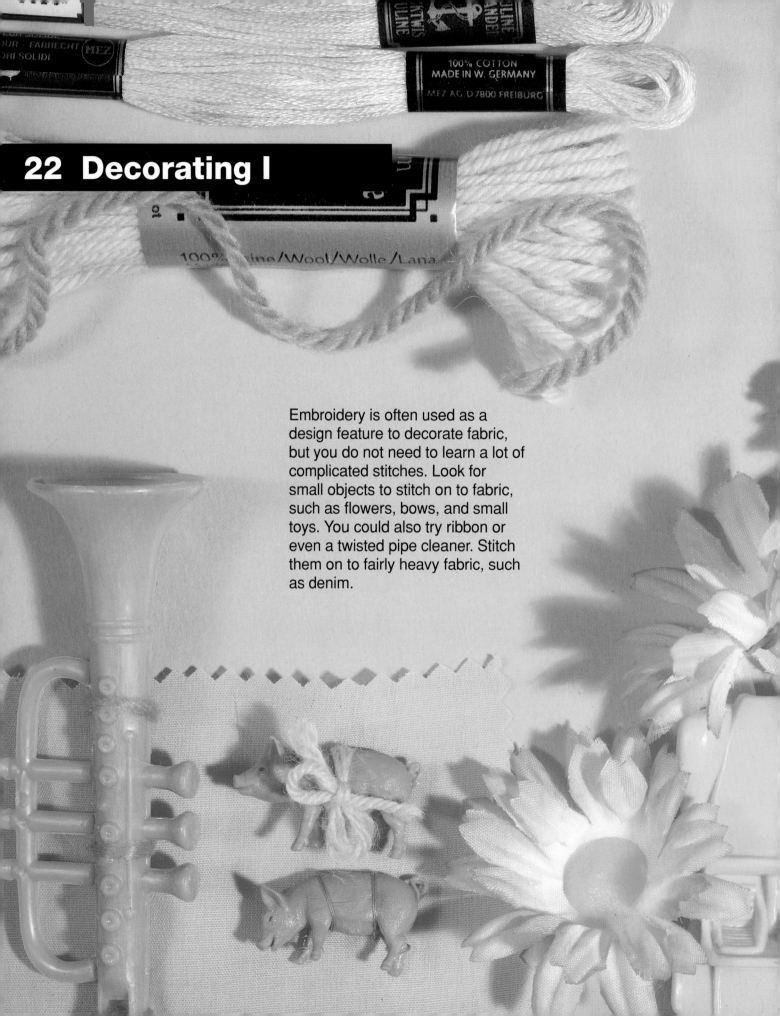

Embroidery is often used as a design feature to decorate fabric, but you do not need to learn a lot of complicated stitches. Look for small objects to stitch on to fabric, such as flowers, bows, and small toys. You could also try ribbon or even a twisted pipe cleaner. Stitch them on to fairly heavy fabric, such as denim.

French knots, like the ones above, are easy to do and give a textured look to fabric or knitting. Use a fairly thick thread so that the bobble really stands out. Pull the needle and thread through to the right side of the fabric. Wind the thread around the needle three or four times. Push the needle and thread back through to the wrong side next to where it came through.

Think of other inventive ways to decorate fabric, but remember that you will have to be very careful when washing the item. In some cases, it would be best to take the objects off first.

24 Decorating II

Using some of the ideas from the previous page, we have created an entire scene using artificial flowers and leaves, plastic ducks, twisted pipe cleaners, and a background of French knots. You can stitch the objects to the fabric, or attach them with fabric glue.

To solve the problem of washing or cleaning a fabric decorated in this way, you can design a garment so that the decorated part can be removed. For example, you could attach a decorated pocket using Velcro or snaps.

When you are tackling a fairly complicated piece of decoration, sketch your idea on paper first.

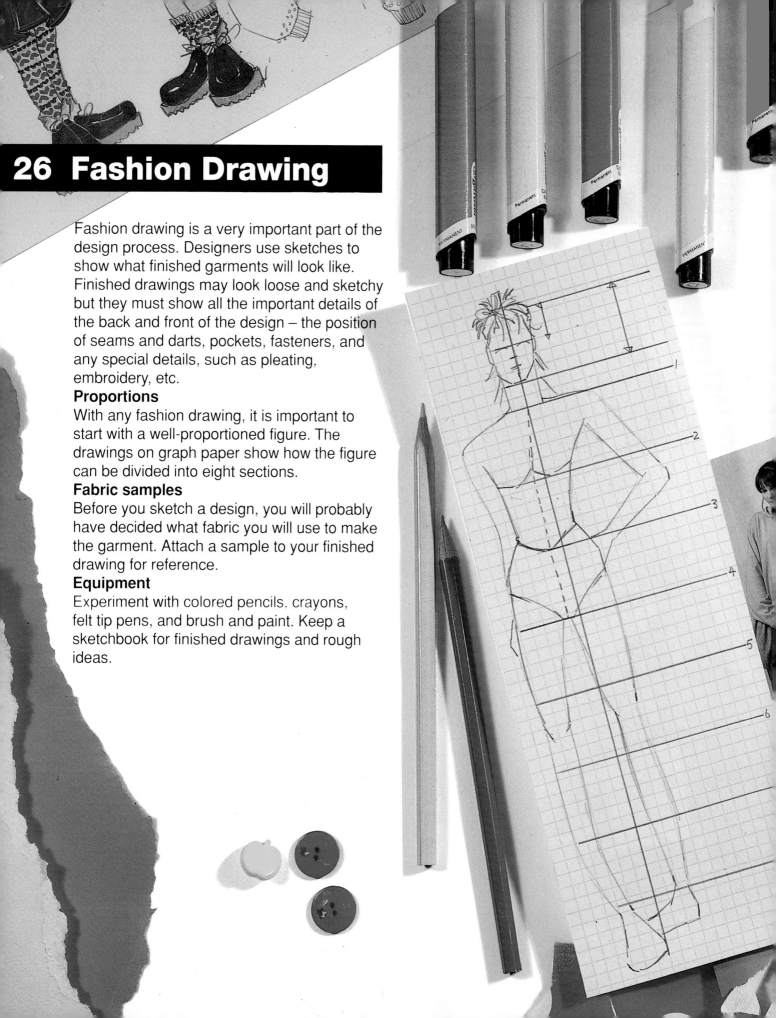

26 Fashion Drawing

Fashion drawing is a very important part of the design process. Designers use sketches to show what finished garments will look like. Finished drawings may look loose and sketchy but they must show all the important details of the back and front of the design – the position of seams and darts, pockets, fasteners, and any special details, such as pleating, embroidery, etc.

Proportions

With any fashion drawing, it is important to start with a well-proportioned figure. The drawings on graph paper show how the figure can be divided into eight sections.

Fabric samples

Before you sketch a design, you will probably have decided what fabric you will use to make the garment. Attach a sample to your finished drawing for reference.

Equipment

Experiment with colored pencils, crayons, felt tip pens, and brush and paint. Keep a sketchbook for finished drawings and rough ideas.

Here are some suggestions for making accessories with no sewing needed. Take a piece of fabric – either square or long and narrow – and twist it around your head. Tie the ends in a knot. Experiment with tying the knots at the side, at the back, and on top.

Think about suitable accessories when you are designing clothes and show them in your original sketches. They might include hats, scarves, bags, belts, gloves, jewelry, and shoes.

Fashions are often inspired by clothes worn in different countries. Take a look at what people wear in China, Africa, and India. What do the fabrics look like? Do they wear accessories? Try adapting these styles with fabrics and accessories that you can find easily, or print your own fabric and make jewelry.

Often, the clothes worn in hot countries are loose and baggy. In many cases, people simply use long pieces of material knotted or belted.

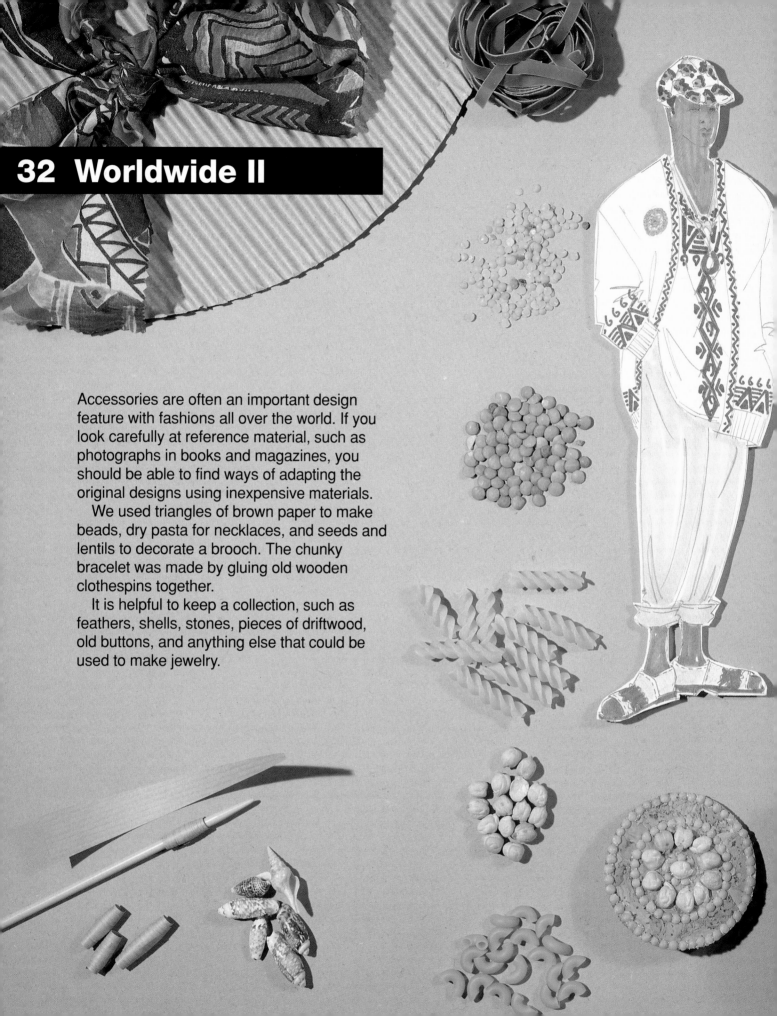

32 Worldwide II

Accessories are often an important design feature with fashions all over the world. If you look carefully at reference material, such as photographs in books and magazines, you should be able to find ways of adapting the original designs using inexpensive materials.

We used triangles of brown paper to make beads, dry pasta for necklaces, and seeds and lentils to decorate a brooch. The chunky bracelet was made by gluing old wooden clothespins together.

It is helpful to keep a collection, such as feathers, shells, stones, pieces of driftwood, old buttons, and anything else that could be used to make jewelry.

Sporty clothes are comfortable, practical, and can be fashionable too. Accessories, such as wrist and headbands, baseball caps, boots, socks, and bags play an important part in the overall look. On the next page you will find some suggestions for putting together your own sporty look. Pick a color scheme and try to coordinate all the elements.

Here are some of the things we used to create our sporty look. Color coordination is important, particularly when so many different elements are used. Keep an eye out for existing accessories that can be adapted.

To make a sporty T-shirt, cut a stencil from cardboard. Put the stencil on a white T-shirt and use a stiff brush to apply fabric paint. Look at the instructions for painting T-shirts on page 18.

In the Past I

Looking at clothes that people have worn through the ages is a good way to get inspiration. Museums, galleries, reference books, and old magazines are all good sources.

You can take elements from the fashions of different years and mix and adapt them to suit the fashion of the moment.

We got our inspiration from many different periods, including the 1960s when bright colors, flowing scarves, and bell-bottoms were all popular.

When you are looking at fashion through history, you will discover that many fashions disappear, only to reappear later in a slightly different form.

40 In the Past II

Often fashions from past years were very elaborate, using lots of fabric and long pieces of lace and ribbons. Many of them were also difficult to wear because they had very full, long skirts and tight bodices. By taking elements from these designs you can create a new look that is more practical for today. For example, you could add lace and ribbons to a plain T-shirt and make a full but short skirt.

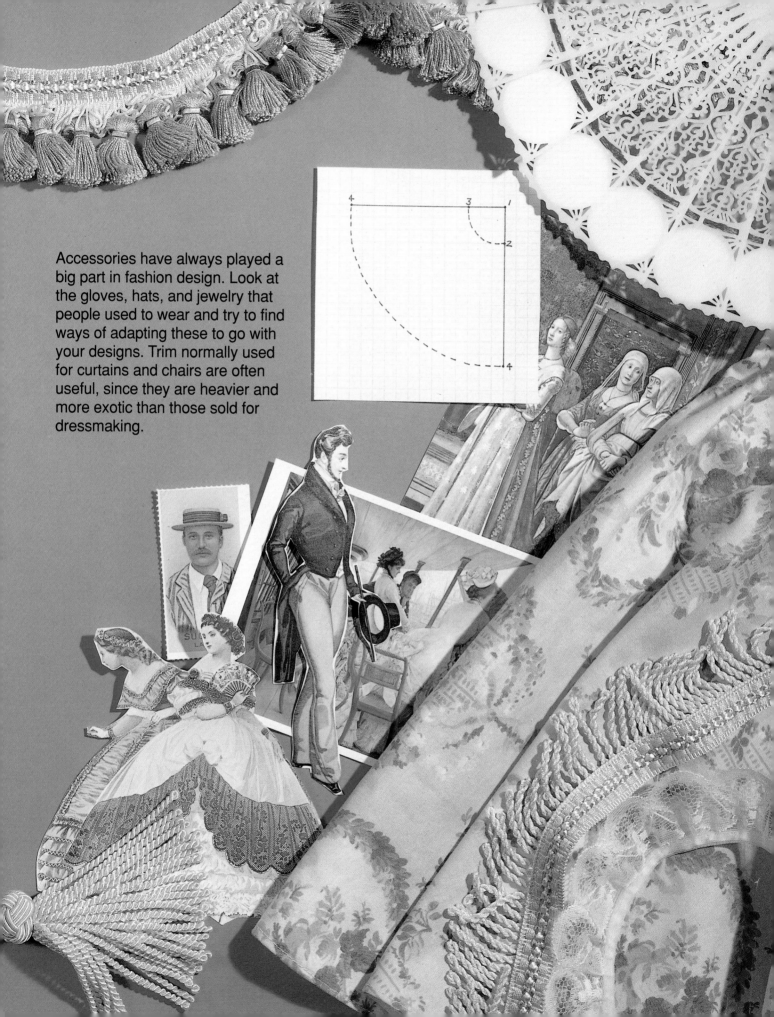

Accessories have always played a big part in fashion design. Look at the gloves, hats, and jewelry that people used to wear and try to find ways of adapting these to go with your designs. Trim normally used for curtains and chairs are often useful, since they are heavier and more exotic than those sold for dressmaking.

42 Second-Hand

Some people never buy new clothes because they are imaginative at adapting old ones. Keep an eye out for yard sales and look in second-hand shops. Wash old clothes well and repair any damage. Using some of the ideas shown in this book – such as embroidery, fasteners, trim, and accessories – turn them into something you will be happy to wear!

Evening clothes are usually very expensive to buy, mainly because of the amount of material and work that goes into making them. But we have designed some beautiful ball gowns that cost next to nothing because they are made from plastic trash bags. The flowers and bows are made from strips cut from sheets of colored cellophane.

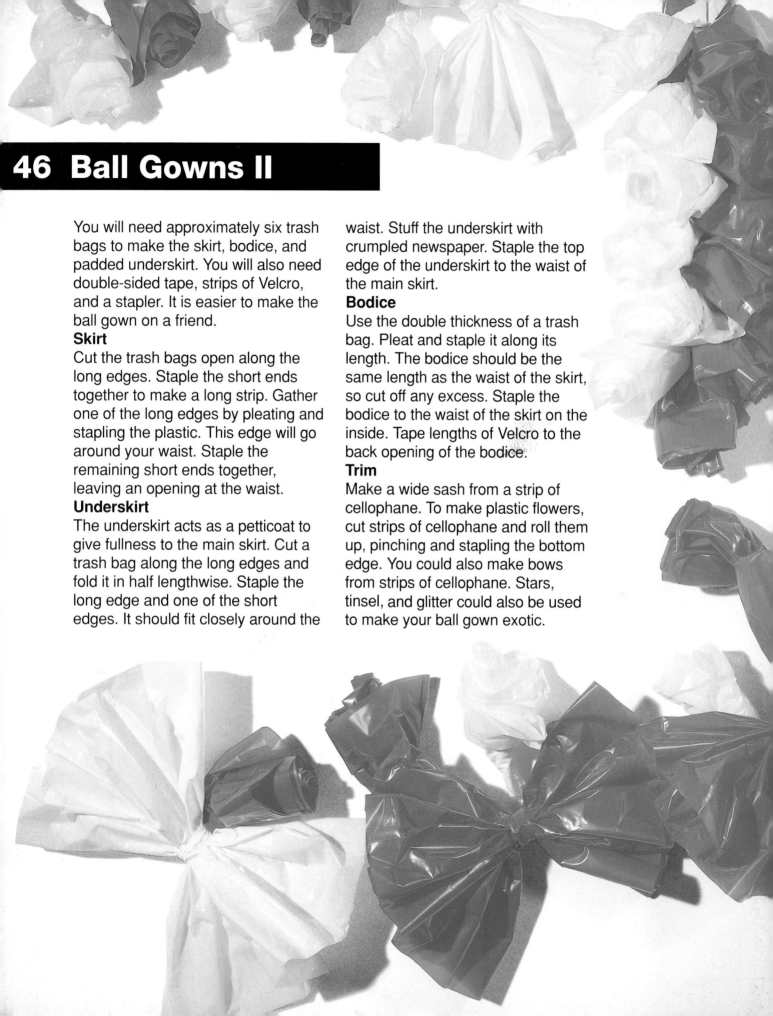

You will need approximately six trash bags to make the skirt, bodice, and padded underskirt. You will also need double-sided tape, strips of Velcro, and a stapler. It is easier to make the ball gown on a friend.

Skirt

Cut the trash bags open along the long edges. Staple the short ends together to make a long strip. Gather one of the long edges by pleating and stapling the plastic. This edge will go around your waist. Staple the remaining short ends together, leaving an opening at the waist.

Underskirt

The underskirt acts as a petticoat to give fullness to the main skirt. Cut a trash bag along the long edges and fold it in half lengthwise. Staple the long edge and one of the short edges. It should fit closely around the waist. Stuff the underskirt with crumpled newspaper. Staple the top edge of the underskirt to the waist of the main skirt.

Bodice

Use the double thickness of a trash bag. Pleat and staple it along its length. The bodice should be the same length as the waist of the skirt, so cut off any excess. Staple the bodice to the waist of the skirt on the inside. Tape lengths of Velcro to the back opening of the bodice.

Trim

Make a wide sash from a strip of cellophane. To make plastic flowers, cut strips of cellophane and roll them up, pinching and stapling the bottom edge. You could also make bows from strips of cellophane. Stars, tinsel, and glitter could also be used to make your ball gown exotic.

INDEX

First published in the United States in 1994 by
Thomson Learning
115 Fifth Avenue
New York, NY 10003

First published in 1991 by Two-Can Publishing Ltd.
Copyright © 1991 Two-Can Publishing Ltd.

Photographs on pages 30, 31 34, 35, 38, 39, 42, 43, 44, 45
copyright © Fiona Pragoff.
All other photographs by Jon Barnes

Library of Congress Cataloging-in-Publication Data

Baker, Wendy
    Fashion/Wendy Baker; author, Diane James.
        p. cm. – (Hands-on)
    "A Two-Can book"
    Includes index.
    ISBN 1-56847-145-9: $16.95
    1. Dressmaking – Juvenile literature. 2. Fashion – Juvenile
    literature. [1. Dressmaking. 2. Fashion] I. James, Diane.
    II. Title. III. Series.
    TT515.B248 1994
    746.9'2–dc20   93-21215

Printed and bound in Hong Kong